DO-IT-YOURSELF

OUTDOOR PROJECTS

OUTDOOR
PROJECTS

Jonathan Edwards

LORENZ BOOKS

This edition is published by Lorenz Books,
an imprint of Anness Publishing Ltd,
Blaby Road, Wigston,
Leicestershire LE18 4SE;
info@anness.com

www.lorenzbooks.com;
www.annesspublishing.com

If you like the images in this book
and would like to investigate using
them for publishing, promotions or
advertising, please visit our website
www.practicalpictures.com
for more information.

Publisher: Joanna Lorenz
Editors: Felicity Forster, Anne Hildyard
Photographers: Peter Anderson, Colin
    Bowling, Jonathan Buckley, Sarah Cuttle,
    John Freeman, Andrea Jones, Debbie
    Patterson & Jo Whitworth
Designer: Bill Mason
Production Controller: Pirong Wang
Additional text: Peter Robinson

PUBLISHER'S NOTE
The author and publishers have made
every effort to ensure that all instructions
contained within this book are accurate and
safe, and cannot accept liability for any
resulting injury, damage or loss to persons
or property, however it may arise. If in any
doubt as to the correct procedure to follow
for any home improvements task, seek
professional advice.

CONTENTS

INTRODUCTION
6

MATERIALS &
TOOLS 8

PAVING, DECKING &
BEDS 20

WALLS, FENCES &
GARDEN STRUCTURES 36

ROCK & WATER
GARDENS 52

INDEX
64

INTRODUCTION

Every gardener knows that there is a lot more to producing a beautiful garden than planting the right species in the right places. Before you can begin to grow plants, shrubs and trees, the ground must be shaped – worked into the right form. Boundaries must be marked, easy access routes to all parts of the garden laid, levels changed and provision made for the future enjoyment of your labours. As a gardener, you need more than just green fingers; you need to be part surveyor, part landscaper, part architect, part carpenter and part builder.

You will need some of the skills of all those professions to create your garden, and since you are unlikely to be able to employ such a variety of

ABOVE: Paving provides much-needed access in the garden, and its harsh edges can be softened with planting.

professionals, you will have no option but to learn the skills yourself. That's not to say that building a garden is a complicated business – it can be, of course, but it doesn't have to be, provided you don't attempt projects that are completely beyond your abilities.

In the process of building a garden, you will have to learn, among many other things, how to mix and lay concrete, how to build walls, how to lay paving, erect fencing, construct a variety of structures from wood, and possibly even create a pond. It is true that some of these jobs require a considerable degree of skill; others, however, are quite simple, and if you are determined to learn and prepared to practise (and accept the occasional failure), you will succeed.

LEFT: Wooden decking provides a durable, practical and easy-to-care-for surface. Ready-made wooden tiles make laying simple.

Although the construction aspect of a garden may seem less attractive to you than the planting, it can be satisfying in its own right. To look at a wall and know that you have built it, or a deck and know that you have designed and constructed it can be very rewarding.

In this book, you will find a variety of projects that will help you build your garden, from simple gravel paving, through fencing, decking and trellis structures, to rock gardens and water features. You can follow them closely or adapt them to suit your own needs.

Don't be afraid to try new skills, or to try again if things don't go quite as you planned first time around. Practice does – nearly – make perfect, and the results will be well worth the effort.

ABOVE: Fences and walls provide an ideal means of supporting climbing plants, or you can train fruit trees along them.

BELOW: Even a small pool can make an eye-catching feature in the garden; when teamed with a rockery, which offers the opportunity of incorporating a cascade, the effect is wonderful.

MATERIALS & TOOLS

Garden projects can involve dealing with a variety of materials. Fortunately, most of the jobs you are likely to encounter are fairly straightforward and rarely require many special tools. Apart from normal gardening tools, you will probably need a few woodworking and masonry tools. Any materials you choose must be rugged enough to withstand weathering. This is particularly true of fixings like nails and screws. Concrete and mortar are commonly found outdoors, too, so an understanding of these materials is essential. Safety is a major consideration when working outdoors, particularly if working from a ladder. If you intend using electric tools, you must take steps to prevent electrocution.

PAVING, DECKING AND BEDS

Hard surfaces are important in your garden, allowing easy access to its various parts and providing a firm "floor" for enjoying the outdoors. They can work in conjunction with raised beds to give the garden form and structure.

PAVING

There is an incredibly wide range of materials suitable for garden paving. Which you choose is largely a matter of personal preference, although each type does have its own advantages and disadvantages. Try to choose a paving material that is sympathetic to the overall design and to the style of your

BELOW: The top row shows (from left to right) natural stone sett, clay paver, brick, artificial sett. The centre row shows a range of the different shapes of concrete paving blocks available. The bottom row shows some of the colours and sizes of concrete paving slabs available.

house. Selecting materials that are already used elsewhere in the garden will help create a co-ordinated effect. Regularly shaped paving works well in a formal setting, whereas paving that consists of smaller units or a range of paving sizes is often a better choice if you are trying to create a more relaxed feel. If you are combining different materials, make sure they are the same thickness to make laying easier.

GRAVEL

One of the big advantages of gravel is that it makes a noise when you walk on it and provides a significant deterrent to potential intruders. It is also good for drives, as it can soak up oil drips from cars without showing permanent stains. However, gravelled surfaces can become weedy and the pieces may blow about. Gravel may also be trodden into the house and develop thin patches.

ABOVE: Gravels naturally vary considerably in colour and size.

DECKING PATTERNS

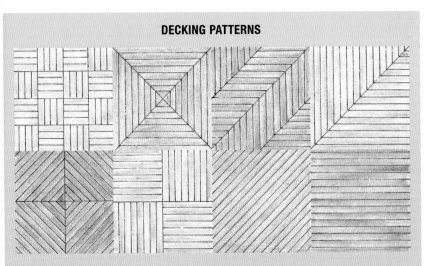

Wooden decking can be laid in a number of decorative patterns. Each style will give your garden a subtly different effect, so consider the pattern carefully before you start. If in doubt, ask a professional designer for help.

DECKING

Decking can be made from hardwood, pressure-treated (tanalized) softwood or plain softwood. Hardwood decks made from white oak or western red cedar are durable and practically maintenance free, but they cost a lot more to construct. Decking made from pressure-treated softwood is less expensive and reasonably durable, but requires seasonal maintenance, while plain softwood decking needs regular maintenance and is prone to rotting, so it is not very durable. Clad the deck with non-slip grooved planks spaced about 6mm (¼in) apart to allow for expansion and to allow water to drain away freely.

BEDS

Traditional permanent raised beds made from bricks or blocks are built in much the same way as solid brick retaining walls.

Raised beds can also be constructed from wood. Old railway sleepers (railroad ties) were traditionally recommended, but designer mini-sleepers are more readily available from garden centres.

ABOVE:
Railway sleepers
(railroad ties) can be used
to make traditional raised beds.

WALL AND FENCE MATERIALS

Mark the boundary of your garden with walls or fencing, which can also define areas within the garden.

WALLS

These can be made from a wide range of materials so can be constructed to suit any style. Substantial or prominent walls, such as those used along the boundary, will fit in more easily with the rest of the garden if they are constructed of the same material used for the house.

BELOW: Bricks come in many colours and finishes, and these are just a small selection of the many available.

ABOVE: Fencing constructed from ready-made panels is popular, and easy and quick to erect. There is a wide choice of styles and panel sizes.

FENCES

The most popular type of fence is the ready-made panel, which comes in various forms, including horizontal lap, vertical lap and interwoven. They are also available in several heights including 1.2m (4ft), 1.5m (5ft) and 1.8m (6ft). Fencing panels are very cheap and easy to put up between regularly spaced, well-anchored posts.

BRICK BONDING

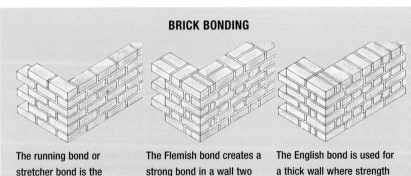

The running bond or stretcher bond is the simplest form of bonding pattern used for walls a single brick wide.

The Flemish bond creates a strong bond in a wall two bricks wide. Bricks are laid lengthways and across the wall in the same course.

The English bond is used for a thick wall where strength is needed. Alternate courses are laid lengthways then across the wall.

POSTS

With all types of fence, the posts should be durable. For preference choose a naturally rot-resistant hardwood, but pressure-treated (tanalized) softwood is more commonly available. With panel fencing the posts are set 1.8m (6ft) apart to accommodate the panel width, but with close-board fencing they are usually spaced more widely – 2.4–3m (8–10ft). Either buy posts that are long enough for the bottom section to be buried into the ground and held firm with concrete, or buy posts the same height as the fence and secure them with fence spikes.

RUSTIC POLES

In an informal or country-style garden, structures made from rustic poles blend naturally into their surroundings. These can be bought as ready-made structures from fencing suppliers or made from fresh-cut wood. Rustic poles are usually roughly jointed and held together with galvanized nails. Rustic structures are not usually as strong as other types and often require more cross-members to improve their rigidity and strength.

If you are using sawn timber for arches and pergolas, choose timber that has been pressure-treated with preservative to prevent it rotting.

SUPPORTS FOR CLIMBING PLANTS

There are several types of support to choose from, but it is important to provide one that matches the size and vigour of the climber it is to support. Against a wall or fence you have the choice of fixing trellis panels, expanding trellis or plastic mesh to the surface or attaching parallel wires.

ABOVE: Rustic poles are ideal in an informal, country-style garden to make open-frame structures such as pergolas and trellises.

ABOVE: Traditional trelliswork made from narrow battens makes a good support for climbing plants against walls or as screening between posts.

ROCK AND WATER MATERIALS

When you build a rock garden, aim as far as possible to create a natural-looking outcrop, otherwise it will take on the appearance of a rock-encrusted heap of soil. The most important ingredient is the rocks, which are more likely to "gel" as a rocky outcrop if they are of the same natural stone. Choose a type of rock that has clear strata lines running through it and an attractive texture and colour. Limestone and sandstone are among the best rock types.

You will need a range of sizes of rock – anything from 15kg (33lb) to 100kg (220lb) – so make sure you have help on hand to manoeuvre the larger stones. If you live near a quarry, use this as your source, otherwise suppliers can be found in local directories; a limited selection of rocks will be offered at some garden centres.

LINING A POND

A pond can be made with a rigid, pre-formed liner or with a special flexible liner. Rigid liners are usually made from plastic or fibreglass, and they come in a range of shapes and sizes to suit most styles of garden. Rigid liners tend to be on the small side, with little space for marginal plants, and are more work to install. A flexible liner, made from PVC, butyl rubber or heavy-duty

ABOVE: White marble cobbles.

ABOVE: York stone.

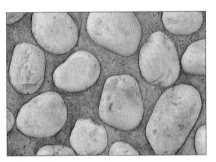
ABOVE: Snowdonian slate.

ABOVE: Welsh green granite.

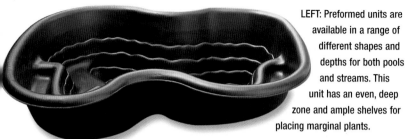

LEFT: Preformed units are available in a range of different shapes and depths for both pools and streams. This unit has an even, deep zone and ample shelves for placing marginal plants.

polythene (polyethylene), gives you a lot more control over the design of your pond. It can be pleated at the corners to fit a rectangular pond, and it is particularly suitable for an informal pond because it can be folded to fit any shape you want. It does, however, require some skill to create a convincingly shaped pond, and the liner can be easily damaged, especially on stony soil.

Although a beginner to water gardening may find a preformed unit tempting because it seems easier to install, such a pond is, in fact, more expensive than a pool of the same size made with the best of the flexible pool liners. In addition, although the units seem huge when they are seen displayed on their sides in a retail centre, they can be disappointingly small when they are dug into the ground.

ABOVE: Flexible pond liners are available in a variety of materials, thicknesses and colours, and are offered with varying guarantees according to quality. Cheaper types can deteriorate when exposed to direct sunlight. An underlay may be necessary on stony ground. From left to right: 1–2 Butyl liner; 3 Low-density polythene (polyethylene); 4 Low-density polythene; 5–9 PVC in different grades; 10 Underlay.

CONCRETE AND MORTAR

Concrete is used to provide a solid and rigid surface as a floor, as paving or as a base for a garage or outbuilding. Mortar is the "glue" that holds the bricks together in a wall. The basis for both concrete and mortar is cement and sand (fine aggregate); concrete also contains stones (coarse aggregate). When mixed with water, the cement sets to bind the aggregates solidly together.

CEMENT

Most cement used around the home is OPC (Ordinary Portland Cement). This is air-setting (that is, moisture in the air will cause it to harden unless bags are kept sealed and in the dry).

BUYING CONCRETE AND MORTAR

There are three ways of buying concrete and mortar: as individual ingredients, as wet ready-mixed and as dry pre-mixed. Buying cement, sand and coarse aggregate separately for concrete is the cheapest option, but you do have to ensure dry storage for the cement. For big jobs, having wet ready-mixed concrete delivered is convenient, provided sufficient manpower is available to transport it from the truck to the site and to level it before it sets. You also need to calculate the quantity needed accurately. For small jobs, bags of dry pre-mix are a good choice: the ingredients are in the correct proportions, and all you do is add water.

CONCRETE AND MORTAR MIXES

CONCRETE	mix	cement	sand	aggregate	yield*	area**
General-purpose	1:2:3	50kg	100kg	200kg	0.15	1.5
		(110lb)	(220lb)	(440lb)	(5.3)	(16)
Foundation	1:2½:3½	50kg	130kg	200kg	0.18	1.8
		(110lb)	(290lb)	(440lb)	(6.4)	(19.4)
Paving	1:1½:2½	50kg	75kg	150kg	0.12	1.2
		(110lb)	(165lb)	(330lb)	(4.2)	(13)

MORTAR	mix	cement	sand	lime***	yield*	bricks laid
Normal	1:5	50kg	200kg	50kg	0.25	850
		(110lb)	(440lb)	(110lb)	(8.8)	
Strong	1:4	50kg	150kg	15kg	0.19	650
		(110lb)	(330lb)	(33lb)	(6.7)	

* cubic metres (cubic feet) per 50kg (110lb) of cement
** area in square metres (square feet) of concrete 100mm (4in) thick
*** or plasticizer are optional - they can be added to the standard mix to improve workability

TOOLS AND EQUIPMENT

Outdoor projects require a variety of tools, depending on the nature of the work. In addition to regular gardening tools, you may need tools for carpentry, bricklaying or paving.

For just about any job, you will need a measuring tape. Many tasks require items to be set perfectly level or vertical, so a spirit (carpenter's) level is essential.

For woodworking, you may need an electric drill together with a hammer and screwdriver for fixings. For brickwork, choose a large trowel for laying mortar and a pointing trowel for finishing joints.

If you are contemplating a moving water feature, you will need a pump. The great majority of pumps now sold are submersible models, which require no more than a connection point near the pool. With the exception of some more recently introduced solar-powered pumps, all pumps run on electricity, either on mains (utility) voltage or on reduced low voltage through a transformer. Modern submersible pumps have an enormous range of outputs. Make sure that you check the running costs if the pump is to be used continuously.

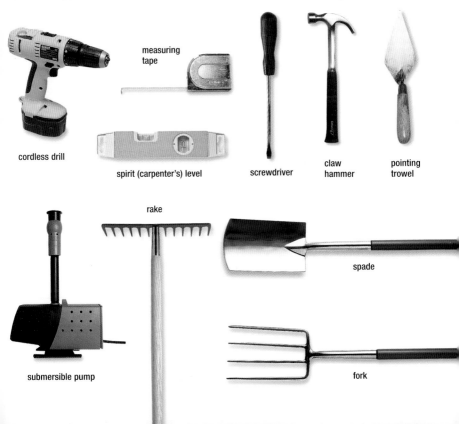

measuring
tape

cordless drill

spirit (carpenter's) level

screwdriver

claw
hammer

pointing
trowel

rake

spade

submersible pump

fork

TOOL MAINTENANCE AND SAFETY

Having invested in a set of good quality tools, it makes sense to keep them in good condition. Not only will they last longer, but they will be easier and more efficient to use. Always keep bladed tools sharp so that they cut efficiently, causing as little damage to the plant tissue as possible. It also makes sense to keep the blades of spades and hoes sharp. When storing tools make sure that all bare metal parts are clean, and have an oily rag to hand so that they can be lightly oiled before being put away. Larger tools such as border forks and spades that

POWER TOOL SAFETY CHECKLIST

Bear in mind that most serious gardening accidents involve powered equipment, so always take extra care during its use.
• Do not attempt to use a power tool unless you are completely sure you can do so safely. Some tools, such as chainsaws, require a skilled operator.
• Read the manufacturer's instructions before you start.
• Never start a job unless you are sure you have time to finish: trying to complete work in a hurry may lead to an accident.
• Check that the equipment is in good working order every time you use it.
• Ensure children and pets are kept well away from the working area.
• Always use the recommended protective clothing and equipment.
• Make sure that the equipment is turned off before moving it around.

USING POWER TOOLS

ABOVE: Always read the safety instructions supplied by the manufacturer carefully before using power tools, and follow them to the letter.

don't have a really sharp edge can be stood in an old bucket of oily sand when they are not needed.

Most garden cutting equipment does not require routine maintenance, other than cleaning and replacing worn blades. If you do intend to use a service centre, to service a petrol (gasoline) machine for example, do it at the end of the season rather than waiting until the centres are busy in the spring, when delays may occur.

WATER SAFETY

It is impossible to make a water garden utterly safe, and this may be a major consideration if the safety of small children is a particular concern. Short of fencing the water off completely and having access through a lockable gate, it is perhaps best to postpone building a dangerously deep pool. A design that allows for the introduction of water at a later date is sensible; you could even use the proposed pool area as a sandpit in the short term.

An existing pool can be made safer by making a safety grid that is strong enough to bear the weight of a child and that will sit just under the surface of the water.

The choice of surfacing near the water's edge also needs careful consideration, particularly when there are elderly people and small children in the garden. Large, flat slabs of natural sandstone can be very dangerous when they are wet and algal growth forms a thin film on the surface. If paving is used, it is advisable to choose one of the concrete paving slabs that are readily available with non-slip surfaces; they are made in a wide range of sizes and colours.

ELECTRICAL EQUIPMENT

The first item of electrical equipment with which you should be familiar is a residual current device (RCD), also known as a contact circuit breaker. Such a device should be considered as a compulsory installation rather than an optional extra to ensure peace of mind. These devices cut off the mains supply within 30 milliseconds of the supply being accidentally earthed, quick enough to prevent a fatal electric shock. They can be purchased for indoor or outdoor installation.

LEFT: A simple plug-in circuit breaker can save a life. Always fit one when working with electric tools.

ELECTRICAL SAFETY

- Never use in the wet.
- Always use an RCD (residual current device) or similar to help prevent accidental electric shocks.
- Only use suitable extension cables (cords) and connectors for outside operation and for the equipment used.
- Make sure extension cables are in good condition and brightly coloured so they are easily seen.
- Never use a damaged cable or connector and always remember to unplug electrical equipment before leaving it unattended.

ABOVE: A home-made, functional grid, just under the surface of the water and covered by cobbles, reduces the danger for small children until they are old enough for the grid to be removed.

PAVING, DECKING & BEDS

Hard surfaces are an integral part of practically every garden; in the form of paths, they allow easy, all-weather access to all the important parts of the plot; as patios and terraces, they provide somewhere to entertain outdoors or simply to sit and enjoy the sights and scents of the garden. Common hard-surface materials include paving slabs, bricks, pavers and gravel. Which you choose depends on the overall garden style and your pocket. For a less harsh appearance, wooden decking is perfect, providing a firm, practical surface that is inexpensive and easy to construct. Many hard surfaces help divide the garden into specific areas; raised beds can do this too, and they bring plants closer to hand.

LAYING PATIOS

A patio provides a smooth, level, hard surface on which to sit and relax and entertain. For these reasons patios are usually best sited in a spot that is not overlooked by neighbours and that is in a convenient position near to the house. If you want to use your patio for sunbathing, it will need to catch the sun for much of the day, and if you want it for entertaining, a site close to the kitchen would be best.

In a north-facing garden, the best place to site a patio may be at the bottom of the garden to catch the maximum amount of sun. It may be more convenient to have two smaller areas of paving: one for sunbathing and one near to the house for entertaining. Wherever you decide to site your patio, make sure that the outlook is pleasing and that it is well screened; the privacy will create a relaxing atmosphere.

DECIDING ON A SIZE

The size of the patio should also be determined by what you want to use it for. To accommodate a standard patio set of table and four chairs, you would need a paved area at least 3 x 3m (10 x 10ft), but preferably larger, about 4 x 4m (13 x 13ft), so that there is room to walk around the furniture while it is in use. However, in a small garden, the patio can dominate the space and create an unbalanced effect in the overall design. In this case, you may be better off paving the whole garden and using planting pockets, raised beds and containers to provide visual interest.

1 Excavate to a depth that will allow for about 5cm (2in) of compacted hardcore (rubble) topped with 2.5–5cm (1–2in) of mixed aggregate, plus the thickness of the paving and mortar.

4 Use a spirit (carpenter's) level placed over more than one slab to ensure that the slab is level. Use a small wedge of wood under one end of the level to create a slight slope over the whole area if necessary. Tap the slab down further, or raise it by lifting and packing in more mortar.

2 On top of the layers of hardcore and aggregate, put five blobs of mortar where the slab is to be placed – one at each corner, and the other in the middle.

3 Position the slab carefully, bedding it down firmly on the mortar. Over a large area of paving, create a slight slope in one direction to allow rainwater to run off freely.

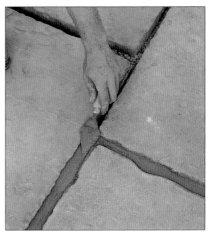

5 Use spacers of an even thickness, such as scraps of wood, to ensure regular spacing between the paving slabs. Remove these later, before the joints are filled with mortar. When you have completed laying the slabs, leave the paving for a day or two for the mortar to set.

6 When the mortar is set, go over the paving again to fill in the joints. Use a small pointing trowel and a dryish mortar mix. Finish off with a smooth stroke that leaves the mortar slightly recessed. This produces an attractive, crisp look. Brush any surplus mortar off the slabs before it dries.

LAYING BRICK AND BLOCK PATHS

Paths exert a strong influence on the design and sense of movement in a garden, so consider the effect during the planning process.

A path's design should reflect the overall theme of the garden. In a formal setting, straight paths with clean lines will reinforce the formality of the design, whereas in an informal garden gently meandering paths will be more appropriate. Calm the feeling of movement by adding changes in direction along the path, and create a sense of mystery by allowing the path to disappear from view – behind a garden structure or border, for example.

LAYING PAVERS

1 Excavate the area and prepare a sub-base of about 5cm (2in) of compacted hardcore (rubble) or sand-and-gravel mix. Set an edging along one end and side first. Check that it is level, then lay the pavers on a bed of mortar.

2 Once the edging is set, lay a 5cm (2in) bed of sharp sand over the area. Use a straight-edged piece of wood to level the surface. Position the pavers, butting them tightly to the edging and to each other.

3 Brush loose sand into the joints of the pavers with a broom. Hire a flat-plate vibrator to consolidate the sand or tamp the pavers down with a club hammer used over a piece of wood.

4 Brush in more sand and repeat the vibrating process. To avoid damage do not go too close to an unsupported edge with the vibrator. The path should be ready to use straight away.

LAYING GRAVEL PATHS

Gravel paths are simple to construct on firmed soil with an underlay of membrane. They can be made any shape, including complicated curves. Little maintenance is required apart from removing the odd weed and raking occasionally to keep it looking neat. Unfortunately, the gravel tends to be kicked into nearby borders and may be walked into the house.

NEAT EDGING

For a period garden, Victorian-style rope edging looks appropriate. You can use it either to retain a gravel path or as an edging to a paved path. Alternatively, waving edgings can be used in a modern setting to create a formal effect.

1 Excavate the area to a depth of about 15cm (6in), and ram the base firm. Provide a stout edge to retain the gravel. For a straight path, securing boards by pegs about 1m (3ft) apart is an easy and inexpensive method.

2 Spread out a layer of compacted hardcore (rubble). Then add a mixture of sand and coarse gravel (sold as combined aggregate). Rake level and tamp or roll until firm.

3 Top up to within 2.5cm (1in) of the edge or boards with the final grade of gravel. In small gardens, the size often known as pea gravel looks good and is easy to walk on. Rake the gravel level.

LAYING A PEBBLE PATIO FEATURE

Create an outdoor "fireside rug" from pebbles, broken garden pots and old china ginger-jar tops. Choose a simple design that is not difficult to achieve; you can always add to it as your confidence grows. The "rug" will make an appealing, witty motif in any paved patio or terrace.

PREPARATION

The bed on which the "rug" is to be set should be prepared to a depth of about 10cm (4in), allowing a 5cm (2in) clearance below the level of the rest of the paving. Dig out the area to the dimensions of the panel and to a depth of 15cm (6in). Mix equal parts of fine aggregate and cement. Then, using a watering can, dribble in water a little at a time until you have a dry, crumbly mix. Use this mix to fill the area, leaving a 5cm (2in) clearance. Level and allow the mix to dry. Gather together plenty of materials for the design and lay them out for size on the dry bed before you begin. Using tile nippers, cut off the bottoms of at least six terracotta pots and snip off the rims in sections. Choose pebbles and slates that are long enough to be wedged in at least 2.5cm (1in) below the surface of the "rug".

You can use a variety of other materials for this kind of decorative feature, such as clay tiles, glass marbles, shells – in fact, anything that is hard and durable. Just use your imagination. Lay out the items "dry" first to determine the best arrangement.

1 Prepare the mortar bedding by mixing equal quantities of sharp sand and cement. Add mortar colour and mix in well. The design is worked while the mortar mix is dry, to enable you to change it if necessary. But the whole design must be completed in a day because moisture from the atmosphere will begin to set the mortar.

4 Brush mortar over the worked areas to make sure that any gaps are filled. To build up the border design, continue working towards the centre, carefully tapping in the pebbles and pieces of slate and terracotta. In this case, china pot lids were added to provide splashes of colour in the four corners.

2 Pour the dry mixture on to the flat bed and, using a straight edge, smooth it out until it is level with the rest of the paving. Then remove a small quantity of the mix from the centre so that it does not overflow as you work. This extracted mix can be put back at a later stage as required, when the design begins to take shape.

3 Plan the edge design by arranging pebbles, pieces of slate and rim sections from terracotta pots around the outside edge of the "rug" until you have achieved a level, decorative border design. Working in towards the centre, gently tap the pieces down into the mortar mix with a hammer.

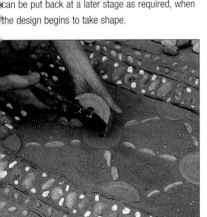

5 Plan the design of the central portion of the "rug" using the bases of terracotta plant pots, pebbles and pieces of slate. Make sure the central area of mortar is level before you begin inserting the pieces. Using tile nippers, cut the sections of terracotta to size, then gently tap everything into position.

6 When the pattern is complete, carefully brush the mortar around the decorative pieces so that there are no gaps between them and the mix. Then use a watering can fitted with a fine rose just to dampen the surface. As the mortar mix absorbs the moisture, it will set hard, fixing the pattern permanently.

LAYING DECKING

Garden decking is a popular choice these days and in many situations is often the best option. It can be cheaper and easier to construct than paving, especially on a sloping site, and provides a hard, flat surface that is functional and looks good too.

Different designs can be achieved by fixing planks in different ways, but on the whole, it is best to keep any pattern fairly simple. In some countries there are building codes that may have to be met. If in doubt, seek professional help with the design, even if you intend to construct it yourself.

CHOOSING A DECK

The easiest way to create a deck is to use ready-made decking tiles that can be laid straight on to a firm, flat surface, such as an old patio, roof terrace or firmed hardcore (rubble). For a better result, lay the tiles on top of a framework of pressure-treated (tanalized) timber and treat any cut ends or joints with wood preservative. You can also buy decks in kit form, and these are very easy to put together and a good choice where the deck isn't fitted into a particular space, such as an island deck part-way down the garden.

Custom-made decking, supplied and fitted by a specialist company, is the most convenient but most expensive option. Such suppliers will take on the whole process, from planning, checking local planning (zoning) regulations and getting the permissions necessary to constructing the deck.

1 Level the area, then use bricks or building blocks to support your decking. Calculate the position of each row. Each timber bearer should be supported in the middle as well as the ends. Excavate the soil and position the blocks.

4 Use wood preservative on the bearers if necessary. Space out the bearers on the block supports. Add extra bearers near the ends and sides of the decking, where the decking will need extra support.

2 Position each block so that about half of it sits in the soil – it is important that air circulates beneath the bearers. Tap down each block to ensure it is level and bedded firmly, adding or removing soil if necessary.

3 Use a spirit (carpenter's) level to ensure that the blocks are level. If the ground is unstable, set the bricks or blocks on pads of concrete. Making sure that they are level is essential, otherwise the final decking will not be stable.

5 Your bearers may not be long enough to stretch the whole length of the deck, in which case make sure joints are made above a block. Use a damp-proofing strip between each block and bearer to prevent water seeping up.

6 Add a plastic sheet to suppress weeds, then saw the decking planks to size and treat with a preservative. Fix in position with galvanized nails leaving gaps of about 6mm (¼in) between planks to allow for expansion.

MAKING GRAVEL BEDS

Sometimes an existing garden can be transformed into a low-maintenance one simply by replacing the lawn. This is especially worth considering if the physical effort of mowing is a problem or if it is too time-consuming.

Not everyone wants to be involved in a major redesign in order to reduce the amount of time and effort spent on the garden. It may be possible to change a few labour-intensive features, and the lawn is often a priority in this respect. For example, you could leave existing beds where they are, lift the grass and replace it with gravel. Even though weeding and dead-heading would still be demanding at times, the chore of mowing the lawn would be eliminated. To prevent gravel spreading on to the surrounding beds, you would need to add an edging to keep it in place.

IN REVERSE

If you consider that a garden simply isn't a proper garden without a lawn, but are not too concerned about lots of flowerbeds to look after, you could keep the grass and fill the beds or borders with gravel instead. This will also suppress weeds in the beds. To reduce the amount of grass that needs mowing, it may be worth cutting some new beds into the lawn.

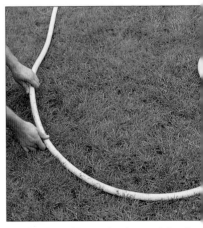

1 Start by marking out the shape and size of the bed with a length of rope, garden hose or sand sprinkled where the outline should be. Make adjustments until you are happy with the look. Oval-shaped beds are ideal for small gardens.

4 If you want to plant through the gravel, loosen the soil in the bed and fork in a generous quantity of well rotted manure or garden compost (soil mix), together with a slow-release fertilizer. Rake the soil level.

2 Cut the outline of the new gravel bed in the turf, working along the hose, rope or sand trail. Ideally, use a half-moon edger, as shown, but if you don't have an edging tool, you can achieve the same result with a spade.

3 Lift the turf from within the outline, digging down to a depth of about 10cm (4in), using a spade. This allows you to add about 8cm (3in) of gravel, well below lawn level so that the chippings do not spread on to the grass.

5 Allow the compost to settle before adding the gravel or firm it by treading it down. Then spread a 5–8cm (2–3in) layer of your chosen gravel evenly over the firmed surface, and level it carefully with a rake.

6 Gravel beds are best planted sparsely, allowing plenty of space between the plants. Try adding a few stones or pebbles here and there to enhance the effect. The result is attractive and easy to care for.

MAKING RAISED BEDS

Although they are time-consuming and expensive to build, raised beds can solve a range of gardening problems, such as poor soil or bad drainage. They are also useful for adding interest to flat plots or for providing level ground in sloping gardens.

DESIGNING WITH RAISED BEDS

Raised beds can be made from bricks mortared together, with "weep holes" (vertical joints free of mortar) every metre (yard) along the base of each wall to allow water to drain out, or they can be constructed from wood such as mini-sleepers (railroad ties). In small gardens they can be combined with paving to produce an intimate courtyard garden. A raised bed can be a functional square or rectangle, or designed to fit a corner in the garden.

CHOOSING THE RIGHT SOIL

Raised beds hold a lot more soil than containers, so they are much easier to look after and you can grow much bigger plants. They also offer the opportunity to grow plants in your garden that otherwise would fail to thrive. For example, if your soil is poor or badly drained, raised beds can be filled with good quality imported loam. Indeed, if you fancy growing plants that

MAKING A RAISED BED USING BRICKS

1 Mark out the shape of the bed using short pointed stakes and string. Use a builders' set square (triangle) to ensure the correct angles. Define the lines with a thin stream of fine sand or use line-marker paint.

4 Clean up the mortar joints while still wet, using a pointing trowel to produce a neat finish. Leave the mortar to harden.

like a specific type of soil, such as acid-loving rhododendrons, raised beds filled with ericaceous compost (soil mix) will provide that opportunity even if your garden soil is not suitable.

The soil in raised beds warms up more quickly than garden soil, so you can start off new plants earlier in spring. Moreover, for anyone who finds bending difficult, raised beds are particularly welcome.

2 Dig out along the markings to a depth of 30cm (12in) and width of 15cm (6in). Fill with concrete to within 5cm (2in) of the top. Firm down, level and leave for 24 hours to set. For concrete, use 1 part cement to 4 parts combined aggregate.

3 Mix some mortar and build up four or five courses of bricks, checking frequently with a spirit (carpenter's) level that the courses are level and the walls of the bed vertical. Check, too, that the sides meet at right angles.

5 Before filling the raised bed with soil, coat the inside of the walls with waterproof paint to prevent moisture from damaging the bricks.

6 Put in a layer of hardcore (rubble) topped with gravel for drainage. Fill with topsoil and stir in a layer of a good potting medium.

7 Make sure the soil is 2.5–5cm (1–2in) below the top of the walls. Then plant up the raised bed in the usual manner, watering in well.

8 The completed bed. In this case, it has been planted with a selection of culinary herbs and wild strawberries.

MAKING A RAISED BED USING WOOD

1 Set the log edging in position and tap it into place. Check with a spirit (carpenter's) level. If you are using flexible edging, drive in stakes to which you can nail the edging.

2 Where the bed has a rectangular shape, as here, you can simply fix the wooden panels together at the corners, using galvanized nails. Drill pilot holes first to avoid splitting the wood.

3 Fill with soil, ensuring that you create the correct conditions for the types of plant you are intending to grow. In this example heathers will be planted; they will need an acid soil.

4 Plant up the raised bed and water in the plants well. Mulch the soil with a thick layer of shredded bark or gravel to retain moisture and discourage weed growth.

MAKING A HERB WHEEL

Herb wheels are charming and popular features that display herbs to their best advantage. They are sometimes made out of old cart or wagon wheels, but these are not easy to obtain. It's far easier to adapt the concept and make a brick "wheel".

The larger the "wheel", the more "spokes" you can introduce. Allocate a contrasting colour, scent or leaf shape to each bed within the spokes to give definition to the wheel. Because most herbs are low growing, the walls of the wheel need not be very high.

1 Use string and canes to mark a circle, then measure off equal points on the circumference for the spokes. Sink a length of earthenware sewage pipe in the centre. Trace over the whole design with fine sand or line-marker paint.

2 Prepare the footings for the walls of the wheel by digging trenches that follow the outline marked on the ground. Fill these with a dry concrete mix. This will provide a firm base for the brickwork.

3 Build the rim and spokes of the wheel with one or two courses of bricks. Set them out dry first to determine whether or not you will need to cut bricks to fit. If you do, use a bolster (mason's chisel) and club hammer, placing the brick on a bed of sand first. Remember to maintain a bonding pattern in the brickwork.

4 Fill in the sections of the wheel and the earthenware pipe with rubble and gravel to provide drainage. Then add topsoil. Plant up the herb wheel with a selection of culinary herbs, such as sage, thyme, rosemary and lemon verbena. Water in well and add an organic mulch. Continue to water until the herbs are established.

WALLS, FENCES & GARDEN STRUCTURES

Walls and fences perform a valuable role in the garden: not only are they useful for marking the boundary of your property and providing essential security, but they can also be used to create positive divisions between specific parts of the garden. While the construction of tall walls requires some skill, low walls can be tackled by the proficient do-it-yourselfer. Fences, on the other hand, require much less skill to erect, particularly if ready-made panels are used. These come in various styles and sizes. Other garden structures you will find useful include pergolas and arches, open-frame constructions that are ideal for supporting climbing plants. You can make them yourself or buy them in kit form.

BUILDING BRICK WALLS

Although walls are mainly thought of as structures to provide security and privacy along the boundary, they are also useful within a garden for building terracing on a sloping plot as well as a range of other features, including raised beds, barbecues, garden screens, seats and plinths for containers and ornaments.

RETAINING WALLS

Solid retaining walls are made from bricks or blocks mortared together. The wall will have to be strong enough to hold back the weight of the soil behind it. For this reason, always use the double-brick construction method, but this time lay the foundations and build the wall so that it slopes back slightly. Leave weep-holes (vertical joints free of mortar) every metre (yard) or so along the base of the wall to allow water to drain out from the soil. Pack in rubble behind the weep-holes and cover with coarse gravel to prevent soil washing out and to stop the weep-holes from becoming blocked with soil.

Dry-stone walls also make good retaining walls up to 1m (3ft) high. Again, the wall needs to be built so that it leans back slightly. The blocks should be selected so that they interlock as much as possible, leaving few gaps. Pack rubble behind the wall as you go to help secure each layer. Large crevices can be filled with suitable plants.

Retaining walls provide an excellent opportunity to experiment with climbers and wall shrubs.

1 All walls require a footing. For a low wall this is one brick wide; for larger, thicker walls the dimensions are increased. Dig a trench 30cm (12in) deep and put 13cm (5in) of rammed hardcore (rubble) in the bottom. Drive pegs in so that the tops are at the final height of the foundation. Use a spirit (carpenter's) level to check they are level.

4 For subsequent courses, lay a ribbon of mortar on top of the previous row, then "butter" one end of the brick to be laid.

2 To form the foundations, fill the trench with a concrete mix of 2 parts cement, 5 parts sharp sand and 7 parts 2cm (¾in) aggregate, and level it off with the top of the pegs. Use a straight-edged board to tamp the concrete down and remove any air pockets. Leave the concrete foundation to harden for a few days.

3 Lay the bricks on a bed of mortar, adding a wedge of mortar at one end of each brick as you lay them for the vertical joints. For a single brick wall with supporting piers, the piers should be positioned at each end and at 1.8–2.4m (6–8ft) intervals, and can be made by laying two bricks crossways.

5 Tap level, checking constantly with a spirit level to make sure that the wall remains level and vertical as it grows.

6 The top of the wall is best finished off with a coping of suitable bricks or with special coping stones sold for the purpose.

ERECTING PANEL FENCES

One of the most popular choices for marking boundaries, fences offer instant privacy and security. They are less expensive to construct than walls and need less maintenance than hedges.

DESIGNING WITH FENCES

There is a huge selection of fencing styles in a range of different materials, including various woods, metals and plastic, so you should have no problem finding a style that will enhance your garden. In the front garden, fences with a more open structure are often used. Examples include picket or post-and-rail fences, ranch-style fences and post-and-chain fences. They do not provide privacy or much security, but they are an attractive way of marking the boundary.

In most back gardens, a boundary fence should recede from view, so choose something robust enough to support climbers and wall shrubs that will help disguise it. However, in certain circumstances you might want to make a feature of a fence. Painting with a wood stain used elsewhere in the garden or to co-ordinate with a planting scheme will emphasize its presence.

1 Post spikes are an easier option than excavating holes and concreting posts in position. Use a special tool to protect the spike top, then drive it in with a sledge-hammer. Check with a spirit (carpenter's) level to ensure it is vertical.

4 Lift the panel into place, supporting its free end with a scrap of wood, and fix it in position by driving galvanized nails through the holes in the brackets. Insert the post at the other end, add more clips and nail the panel to it.

PLANNING PERMISSION

Check with your local planning (zoning) authority before erecting a new wall or fence. Normally, you require planning consent for any fence more than 1.8m (6ft) high and for a fence more than 1m (3ft) high that abuts a highway.

2 Insert the post in the spike, checking that it is vertical again, then lay the panel in position on the ground and mark the position of the next post. Drive in the next spike so that it abuts the panel, testing for the vertical again.

3 There are various ways to fix the panels to the posts, but panel brackets are the simplest. Simply nail a pair of these galvanized U-shaped brackets to each post, either aligning them with one edge or the centre.

5 Always check that each panel is level before making the final fixings, using a spirit level. Check too that the tops of the panels are in line, unless you are working on a sloping site and are stepping them.

6 Finish off by nailing a cap to the top of each post. This will keep water out of the end grain of the timber and extend its life. Wooden and plastic caps are available, some incorporating decorative finials.

ERECTING RANCH-STYLE FENCES

anch-style fences consist of broad horizontal rails fixed to stout upright posts. They are usually quite low, and frequently consist of just two or three rails. White-painted wood is a popular material, but wipe-down plastic equivalents are very convincing and easy to maintain. For a small garden they provide a clear boundary without becoming a visual obstruction. Also, rain and sun shadows are not created in the way that occurs with solid fences.

1 The posts of a ranch-style fence must be well secured in the ground. Use 10cm (4in) square posts, set at 2m (6ft) intervals. For additional strength, add 8cm (3in) square intermediate posts. Make sure the posts go at least 45cm (18in) into the ground. Concrete the posts into position, then fill in with soil.

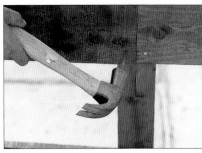

2 Screw or nail the boards in place, making sure that the fixings are galvanized to protect them against rust. Use a spirit (carpenter's) level to check that the boards are horizontal. Butt-join them in the centre of a post, but try to stagger the joints on each row so that there is not a weak point in the fence.

3 Fit a post cap to improve the appearance and also protect the posts. Paint with a good quality paint recommended for outdoor use. Choose the colour of the paint carefully; you will need to keep white paint clean if the fence is to remain looking good.

ABOVE: Low ranch-style fences are ideal as less obtrusive boundary markers where the security of a tall solid fence is not required. When weathered, they can merge into the background, helping to delineate the landscape without overwhelming it.

CONSTRUCTING TRELLIS ARBOURS

Trellises can be used to divide the garden into separate "rooms" and add a strong vertical dimension to an otherwise flat garden scheme. If you are looking for a more subtle application, a trellis can provide a secluded corner for a garden seat, creating a peaceful sitting area or arbour.

The upright trellis arbour shown here can be adapted if you want to erect an overhead trellis. For a 200cm (6ft) long arbour, you will need the following panels of lattice (diagonal) trellis: three panels, 200 x 60cm (6 x 2ft); two panels, 200 x 30cm (6 x 1ft); one concave panel, 200 x 45cm (6 x 1½ft); and one panel, 200 x 90cm (6 x 3ft). You will require six wooden posts, 8 x 8cm (3 x 3in), each 2.2m (7ft) long, and six post spikes.

1 The 200 x 60cm (6 x 2ft) panels are for the sides and top. The two narrow panels and concave panel are for the front, and the remaining panel is used horizontally across the top of the back. Trim the posts to length, making each of them 200cm (6ft) plus the depth of the socket in the post spikes.

2 Start with each back panel. Mark the post positions 200cm (6ft) apart and drive in post spikes. Insert a post into each spike socket. Using 5cm (2in) nails, temporarily fix the top of the trellis to the tops of the posts. Drill clearance holes for 5cm (2in) No.10 rust-proof screws down each side of the trellis. Drive in the screws.

3 In the same way, position the front outside posts and fix the side panels, then the inside front posts and front panels. Fix the concave panel into the panels on each side of it. Finally, fix the roof in position, screwing it into the posts. Paint the arbour with exterior decorative wood stain and leave to dry.

ASSEMBLING ARCHES

Arches are not only quick and easy to construct, but also, if correctly positioned, can effectively transform the appearance of a garden. Flatpack kits are now available in a variety of materials and styles to suit both traditional and contemporary gardens.

DESIGNING WITH ARCHES

Arches can perform several functions in the garden. They look lovely when positioned over a path and festooned with colourful climbing plants. Ideally, the structure should frame a distant object, such as an ornament, or focus the eye on the path as it leads tantalizingly out of sight into the next area of the garden. Arches can also be used to link borders on each side of the garden to give the overall design a feeling of coherence.

Although an arch will stand quite effectively on its own as a decorative feature in its own right, you can also incorporate one into a fence or open-frame screen (such as trellis or rustic poles) that acts as a divider between one part of the garden and another, adding greater interest to the access point. Another possibility is to erect a series of arches along a path to create an airy tunnel effect, which would create interesting patterns of shade and light and be particularly effective if fragrant climbing plants were allowed to clamber over them.

Many kit arches are made from trellis panels, which are simply nailed together, and a typical example is shown here.

1 The simplest way to make an arch is to use a kit, which only needs assembling. First, establish the post positions, allowing a gap between the edge of the path and each post, so that plants do not obstruct the path.

4 The next stage is to construct the overhead beams of the arch. Lay both halves on a large flat surface and carefully screw the joint together at the correct angle. Use rust-proof screws to prevent them becoming weakened by corrosion.

2 Dig four 60cm (2ft) deep holes to hold the posts. Alternatively, choose a kit with shorter posts for use with fence spikes. Drive the spikes in with a special tool, using a spirit (carpenter's) level to ensure they are vertical.

3 Position the legs of the arch in the holes. Backfill with the excavated earth and compact with your heel. Check that the legs are vertical using a spirit level. If using spikes, insert the legs and then tighten any securing bolts or screws.

5 Fit the overhead panels for the arch to the posts. In this example, they simply slot into the tops of the posts and are nailed in place. Use galvanized nails, which will resist corrosion when exposed to the elements.

ABOVE: The completed arch provides an interesting focal point in the garden. It can be left like this to stand on its own or be used to support a climbing plant – preferably one that produces fragrant blooms.

MAKING PERGOLAS

A pergola is simply an open-frame structure, often placed over a patio adjacent to the house to create an intimate area for outdoor entertaining. It can be clad in shading materials, or a more natural covering of climbers. Pergolas also can be used away from the house, as a covered walkway along the sunny side of the garden or a point of focus in the middle of the garden.

There are two main styles of wooden pergola: traditional and Oriental. The former has fewer, larger roofing timbers with square-cut ends, while the latter has bevelled ends.

You can also buy plastic-coated tubular metal pergolas. These are lightweight and easy to put up.

ABOVE: If you need to attach a horizontal pole to a vertical one, saw a notch of a suitable size in the top of the vertical one so that the horizontal piece will fit snugly on top.

ABOVE: Use a halving joint where two poles cross. Mark the position of the joint on each pole and make two saw cuts halfway through the pole, then remove the waste wood carefully with a chisel. Fix the two poles together with galvanized nails or screws.

ABOVE: Bird's-mouth joints are useful for connecting horizontal or diagonal pieces to uprights. Cut out a V-shaped notch about 2.5cm (1in) deep and saw the other piece of timber to match the shape. You may need to use a chisel to achieve a good fit.

ABOVE: To join two horizontal pieces of wood, saw two opposing and matching notches so that one sits over the other. Secure the two pieces with galvanized nails or screws.

ABOVE: To fix cross-pieces to horizontals or uprights, remove a V-shaped notch, using a chisel if necessary to achieve a snug fit, then fix in place with galvanized nails.

ABOVE: Try out the assembly on the ground, then insert the uprights in prepared holes and make sure these are secure before adding any further pieces. Most pieces can be nailed together, but screw any sections subject to stress. Use rust-proof screws and nails.

ABOVE: In contrast to traditional rustic poles, this Oriental-style pergola has been made from sawn timbers. Make sure that the timbers are strong enough to take the weight of any climbers and rambling plants that you plan to grow on the pergola.

ERECTING POSTS AND WIRES

The simplest form of support for fruiting canes consists of stout posts at 3m (10ft) intervals along the row with horizontal fencing wire strung between the posts and held taut with tensioning bolts. Only two wires are needed, one running about 60cm (2ft) from the ground, and the second at a height of about 1.2m (4ft). It is important to ensure that the posts are set firmly in the ground, since they must resist the pull of the wire when it is taut. For this reason, the end posts must be reinforced with diagonal braces.

1 Knock a stout post well into the ground at the end of the row of cane fruit. It may be easier to dig a hole and insert the post before backfilling and ramming down the earth. You can hire an auger to keep the hole size to a minimum.

2 Knock in another post at an angle of 45 degrees to the vertical to act as a support to the upright post. Nail firmly using galvanized nails so that the upright post is rigid and will support the tension of tight wires.

3 Fasten the wires around one end post and pull tight along the row, stapling it to each vertical post. Keep the wire as taut as possible. If necessary, use eye bolts on the end posts to tension the wire.

4 Fasten the canes – in this case raspberry canes – to the wires with string or plant ties. Space the canes out evenly along the wires so that the maximum amount of light can reach the leaves to ensure good growth.

ERECTING PILLARS

Many climbers are suitable for training up single posts, often called pillars, although it is probably best to avoid very vigorous climbers. If space permits, a series of pillars can be erected along a path, linked garland-fashion by chunky rope along which climbers can grow. Climbers also look effective trained up tripods or, alternatively, you can make your own supports from canes.

Whichever freestanding support you choose, it is essential that it is anchored securely into the ground. This means digging a deep hole and ramming down the infill around the post. It may even be necessary to concrete the support into the ground. Check that it remains vertical while you do this.

1 Dig a hole at least 60cm (2ft) deep. Put in the post and check that it is upright. Backfill with earth, ramming it firmly down as you work. In exposed gardens a more solid pillar can be created by filling the hole with concrete.

2 Plants can be tied directly to the post, but a more natural support can be created by securing wire netting to the post. Self-clinging climbers such as clematis will then be able to climb by themselves with little attention required.

3 Plant the climber a little way from the pole. Lead the stems to the netting and tie them in. Self-clingers will take over, but plants such as roses will need to be tied in as they grow. Twining plants can be grown up the pole without wire.

FIXING TRELLISES TO WALLS

Climbing and rambling plants can provide an interesting vertical element to the garden and are useful for disguising or concealing less attractive features. There are many different types to choose from, and lots of them produce beautiful, often fragrant, blooms; others are evergreen, offering year-round pleasure.

When choosing a support for a climbing plant, it is important to take into consideration the method by which it climbs. Some climbers, such as ivy, can be grown on a bare brick wall, but most will need a trellis to support them as they grow. For example, climbers such as climbing and rambler roses are not self-clinging and need to be tied in to their supports.

1 The trellis should be sturdy and in good condition. Ensure it has been treated with wood preservative. Take the trellis panel to the wall and mark its position. The bottom of the trellis should be about 30cm (12in) from the ground. Drill holes for fixing the spacers and insert plastic or wooden plugs.

2 Drill matching holes in a wooden batten and secure it to the wall, checking with a spirit (carpenter's) level that it is horizontal. Use wood that will hold the trellis at least 2.5cm (1in) from the wall. Fix another batten at the base, and one halfway up for trellis more than 1.2m (4ft) high.

3 Drill and screw the trellis to the battens, first fixing the top and then working downwards. Check that the trellis is straight using a spirit level. The finished trellis should be secure, so that the weight of the climber and any wind that blows on it will not pull it away from its fixings.

WIRES TO SUPPORT CLIMBERS

Where plants are to be trained up walls or solid fences, stretching horizontal wires across the surface can provide an effective means of supporting them, particularly if they need to be tied in to the supports. On a fence, the wires can be secured with galvanized staples driven into the posts, provided the plant is not a vigorous grower likely to produce heavy stems, which might pull them out.

To support trees against walls, use wires held by vine eyes. Depending on the type of vine eye, either knock them into the wall or drill and plug before screwing them in. Pass heavy-duty galvanized wire through the holes in the eyes and fasten to the end ones, keeping the wire as tight as possible.

1 Drill holes in the wall and insert vine eyes to support the wires. If you use vine eyes with a screw fixing, insert wall plugs first. Vine eyes are available in several lengths, the long ones being necessary for vigorous climbers, such as wisteria, that need wires further from the wall.

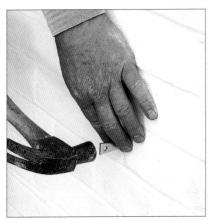

2 The simplest vine eyes are wedge-shaped. Hammer them directly into the masonry and then feed the wire through holes. Although wedge-shaped eyes are suitable for brick and stone walls, the screw type are better for wooden fences and posts.

3 Thread galvanized wire through the hole in the vine eye and wrap it around itself to form a firm fixing. Thread the other end through the intermediate eyes, set at no more than 2m (6ft) intervals and preferably closer, and fasten the wire around the end eye, keeping it as taut as possible.

ROCK & WATER GARDENS

Among the many decorative aspects you can add to your garden, rock gardens and water features can make wonderful, eye-catching displays. Neither needs to be particularly large, so even the smallest garden can take advantage of what they have to offer, and each provides the opportunity of growing something different. With the former, you can choose delicate, colourful alpine plants; with the latter, lush water lilies or statuesque marginal plants. Moreover, a water feature will allow you to add movement and the relaxing sound of dappling water if you incorporate a pump to operate a fountain or cascade. Even a simple pebble fountain will bring the benefits of moving water to a patio corner.

BUILDING ROCK GARDENS

Rock gardens benefit from an open site. If planned well, they can each enhance the other. In a level garden the soil excavated during pond installation can be used to form the base.

DESIGNING A ROCK GARDEN

On sloping ground you can build a natural-looking outcrop or a series of terraces, or a combination of the two for a very large rockery. On a level site a more acute outcrop, with strata lines at a 45-degree angle, can work well, or choose a series of flattish stones to create a pavement effect with horizontal strata lines.

Careful planning is essential. Mark out the site using string and improve drainage if necessary – if you have heavy soil this may mean digging a hole 30cm (12in) deep, half-filling it with rubble and covering it with a layer of sharp sand before topping with good, free-draining topsoil.

BUILDING A ROCKERY ON A SLOPE

If practicable, start at the bottom of the slope and build in layers. Choose the best-looking stone to start building your rockery and position it in the middle so that the strata lines angle gently back into the ground. About one-third of each stone will be underground, so you will have to scoop out a hole to accommodate it. Then add stones on each side so that the strata lines fall away at exactly the same angle. Add subsequent layers in the same manner.

1 The base of the rock garden is a good place to dispose of rubble and subsoil excavated during the creation of a pond. On heavy soil, take steps to improve the drainage within the outline of the rock garden.

4 Repeat the process for the next row of rocks, levering them into position. Using rollers and levers is the best way to move heavy rocks around – do not try to lift them. Make sure you have someone on hand to help too.

2 Use a special soil mixture for the top 15–23cm (6–9in), especially if soil excavated from a pond is used. Mix equal parts of soil, coarse grit and peat (or peat substitute) and spread evenly over the mound.

3 Lay the first rocks at the base, making sure that the strata run in the same direction, and add more soil mixture around them. Make sure each stone is set firm before positioning the next by ramming soil around it.

5 As each layer is built up, add more of the soil mixture and consolidate it around each of the rocks in turn. Take care to prevent the creation of voids between the rocks, which could lead to subsidence later on.

6 Make sure that the sides slope inwards and make the top reasonably flat rather than building it into a pinnacle. Position the plants, then cover the exposed soil with a layer of stone chippings to give the appearance of scree.

PONDS WITH FLEXIBLE LINERS

After deciding on the best position for a pond in your garden, you need to consider its style and dimensions as well as the construction materials.

PLANNING A POND

A self-sustaining pond that does not require constant maintenance should be as big as possible. Whatever the shape, it should have at least 5 square metres (54 square feet) of surface area, and so that it doesn't heat up too quickly in summer or get too cold in winter, it also needs to be at least 60cm (2ft) deep over much of that area. A marginal shelf 23cm (9in) wide and about 15cm (6in) below the surface of the water around the edge is needed to accommodate plants that like their roots in water, but their shoots and leaves in the air. Before excavating, check that there are no underground obstructions, such as pipes and cables.

WHAT SIZE FLEXIBLE LINER?

Flexible liners are available in a range of standard sizes. To calculate the size you will need for your proposed pond, use the following formula:

Length = 2 x maximum depth + maximum length of the pond

Width = 2 x maximum depth + maximum width of the pond

For example, a pond that is 3 x 2m (10 x 6ft) with a maximum depth of 50cm (20in) will require a flexible liner that is at least 4 x 3m (13 x 10ft).

1 Mark out the shape of the pond with garden hose or rope for curves, and pegs and string for straight edges. Then remove any turf and start to excavate the pond. Redistribute the topsoil to other parts of the garden.

4 On stony soil, you may need to line the hole further with insulation material or special pond liner underlay. Trim the liner underlay so that it fits neatly into the hole to form a continuous layer without any gaps or voids.

2 Dig the whole area to about 23cm (9in) deep, then mark the positions of the marginal shelves. Each should be about 23cm (9in) wide. Dig the deeper areas to 50–60cm (20–24in) deep. Angle all the sides so they slope slightly inwards.

3 Check the level as you work. Correct discrepancies using sieved garden soil. Make sure there are no sharp stones on the base and sides that might damage the liner, then line the hole with builders' sand.

5 Place the liner into position without stretching it unduly. Choose a warm day as this will make it more flexible. Weigh down the edges with stones, then fill the pond slowly. Ease the liner over the contours as the pond fills.

6 Once the pond is full, trim back the excess liner to leave an overlap of at least 15cm (6in) around the edge. Cover the overlapping liner with paving or other edging. To disguise the liner, overlap the water's edge by 2.5cm (1in).

INSTALLING PREFORMED PONDS

If you would like to have a small, formal pool with a symmetrical shape, a preformed pool unit is ideal. Such a pool is relatively easy to install and you will not have to deal with the bulky folds in tight corners that can be a problem with some of the thicker flexible liners. The stronger preformed units are useful for raised or partially raised pools because the walls are strong enough to support the internal water pressure; a decorative outer wall can be built to disguise the unit.

There are two main types of preformed unit: rigid and semi-rigid. Rigid units are made of fibreglass or thick reinforced plastic; semi-rigid units are thinner and made from a cheaper plastic. Both types are better when they are moulded into simple shapes rather than being too fussy, with narrow outlines and several different levels. The regular shapes make it easier to pave around the edges and to disguise the plastic with a slight overhang of the edge of the paving.

Do not be tempted to skimp on the preparation of the hole, and make sure that the sides and base are evenly supported. The larger units are extremely heavy when full of water and are subject to enormous strain if they are not properly supported. This can result in hairline cracks forming in even the thicker fibreglass units. Greater care is necessary with the plastic preformed units because their sides are less rigid and can bend in any uneven pressure of water and soil.

1 Place the rigid liner in the desired position. Transfer its shape on to the ground by inserting canes around the edge of the unit. Use a garden hose, rope or sand to mark the outline on the ground.

4 Remove any large stones protruding from the bottom and sides. Place the liner in the hole, then add or remove soil as necessary to ensure a good fit so that the liner is well supported. Check with a spirit level that it is level.

2 Remove the unit and canes, and excavate the hole to approximately the required depth, following the profile of the shelves as accurately as possible. Make frequent checks with a measuring tape, or trial-fit the liner.

3 Use a spirit (carpenter's) level and straight-edged board, laid across the rim of the hole, to check that it is level. Measure down from the board to ensure that it is the required depth. Make any necessary adjustments.

5 Remove the pond and line the hole with damp sand if the soil is stony. With the pond in position and levels checked again, backfill with sand or fine soil, being careful not to push the pond out of level.

6 Fill with fresh water and backfill further if necessary as the water level rises, checking the level frequently to make sure the liner has not moved. Allow to stand for a few days before stocking with plants.

BUILDING RAISED POOLS

Raised pools are easier to empty than sunken pools, and they suffer from fewer problems, such as leaves and other plant debris blowing in. They require very little excavation and are an ideal solution on sloping sites. A substantial surround, such as twin walls, is necessary when a raised pool is made with a flexible liner so that it can withstand the internal water pressure, and this makes them more costly to build than sunken pools; if they are built with brick or walling stone, some degree of bricklaying skill will be necessary.

A simple raised pool can be made by installing a rigid preformed unit and surrounding it with a raised edge of several courses of old railway sleepers (railroad ties), secured with brackets. Alternatively, a rigid unit can be raised above the ground according to the height and type of rock edging.

INITIAL PREPARATION

Mark the outline of the shape that the raised wall of sleepers will occupy. Check that the preformed unit will fit inside the outline. Clear the turf and other plants from the ground beneath the position of the pool and rake the soil level. Spread a layer of gravel, 5cm (2in) deep, over the marked-out area. This will prevent the bottom course of sleepers from sitting on wet soil, which could lead to rotting.

1 After marking out and preparing a level site, lay the first course of sleepers (railroad ties) to the shape required. For a rectangle, which will hold a variety of preformed shapes, you will need to cut down half of the sleepers to form the two shorter sides and use a builders' set square (triangle) to check that a true right angle is formed by the sleepers on the short side. A square surround will save considerable cutting. Where possible, butt a cut edge to the inside of a neighbouring sleeper so that it is not exposed.

2 As each course is placed on top of the one before, arrange the sleepers in a bonding pattern so that the joints in one course are overlapped by the sleepers above. This method will provide extra rigidity and strength in the construction. Continue adding courses of sleepers until the correct level for the preformed liner is reached. If the height of the liner is not equal to a whole number of sleepers, add another course so that the surrounding wall is slightly higher than the pool.

3 When sufficient height is reached, spread a 5cm (2in) layer of sand inside the surround to act as a base for the liner. This will make any final levelling of the rigid unit much easier.

4 Make the structure more rigid by screwing galvanized steel angle brackets inside the corners of the surround to connect each sleeper to its neighbour.

5 Extra rigidity will be given by driving in galvanized nails, 15cm (6in) long, from one course of sleepers to the next. Knock the nails in at an angle on the inside edge of the surround so that they are not seen later.

6 Line the inside of the raised bed with cheap polythene (polyethylene) secured to the sleepers by nails. This helps to prevent small mammals like mice from creeping inside the gaps between the sleepers and nesting in the sand.

7 Enlist help to lift the pool inside the sleepers and check that the sides are level. Keep the sides of the pool just lower than the top of the sleeper wall.

8 Add sieved soil between the pool rim and the sleepers. Firm this with a sawn-off broom handle, then level it around the rim. Add small rocks and alpine plants, top-dressed with fine grit.

MAKING A PEBBLE FOUNTAIN

The easiest way to create a small water feature with moving water is to sink a reservoir into the ground so that it is about 5cm (2in) below the surrounding soil. Then create a catchment area for the feature by sloping the soil around the hole towards the reservoir, so that when it is lined with heavy-duty polythene (polyethylene) or a flexible pond liner, water will drain back into the reservoir. Position the pump in the reservoir and cover with heavy-duty steel mesh and smaller mesh to prevent small pebbles from falling through. Arrange cobbles and pebbles on the mesh to hide the reservoir and the catchment area to create a pebble fountain.

You can change the display by adding a millstone or another focal point, or by connecting different types of fountain jet to the outlet pipe of the submerged pump to create all manner of display fountains.

WHAT SIZE PUMP?

The size of pump you require will depend on the amount of water needed to produce the effect you want. A small water feature will require a pump with a flow rate of about 450 litres (about 120 gallons) per hour, while a large fountain will need one that can supply 650 litres (about 170 gallons). If you want to combine features or have a watercourse you will need a much larger pump (see product packaging for details).

1 Mark out the diameter of the reservoir on the ground and dig a hole that is slightly wider and deeper than its dimensions. Place a shallow layer of sand at the bottom of the hole. Ensure the reservoir rim is slightly below the level of the surrounding soil.

4 Replace the plastic sheet over the reservoir, with the fountain pipe protruding through the hole and fit the fountain spout. Check the operation of the pump, adjusting as necessary.

2 Backfill the gap between the reservoir and the sides of the hole with soil. Firm in. Create a catchment area by sloping the surrounding soil slightly towards the rim of the reservoir. Place two bricks at the bottom to act as a plinth for the pump. Then position the pump.

3 Ensure the pipe used for the fountain spout will be 5–8cm (2–3in) higher than the sides of the reservoir. Line the catchment area with a plastic sheet and either cut it so the plastic drapes into the reservoir, or cut a hole in the centre for the fountain pipe. Fill with water.

5 Place galvanized mesh on top to support the weight of large cobbles. If you are using small stones, place a smaller mesh on top of the larger one to prevent them falling through.

6 Cover the area around the pump with a layer of cobbles. Check that the height of the spout is satisfactory. When you are happy with the fountain, finish arranging the cobbles.

INDEX

A
access 6, 10, 21
arches 13, 37, 44–5

B
beds 10
    gravel beds 30–1
    raised beds 11, 21, 32–3,
        34, 38
boundaries 6, 12, 37, 38, 40
bricks 32–3, 38–9, 60
    bonding 12
    herb wheel 35
    paths 24
    paving 10, 21

C
cascades 7, 53
cement 16, 33, 39
circuit breakers 19
climbing plants 38, 44, 45,
    46, 49, 50, 51
concrete 6, 9, 16, 33, 39
    paving 10, 19

D
decking 6, 7, 11, 21
    laying 28–9
drills 17

F
fences 6, 7, 12, 37
    panel fences 40–1
    ranch-style 42
    rustic fences 13, 44
fountains 53, 62–3

G
gravel 7, 10, 21, 30–1, 60
    paths 25

H
hammers 17, 40
hardwood 11, 13
hedges 40
herb wheel 35

L
ladders 9

M
measuring tape 17, 59
mortar 9, 16, 17, 32, 33

N
nails 9, 34, 40, 41, 42, 45,
    46, 47, 48, 61

P
paths 24, 25
patios 21, 22–3, 53
    pebble feature 26–7
paving 6, 19
    paths 24
    pavers 10, 21
pebble fountains 53, 62–3
pergolas 13, 37, 46–7
plants 32, 35, 48, 53, 56
    climbers 38, 44, 45, 46,
        49, 50, 51
ponds 6, 7
    lining 14–15, 56–7
    preformed 14–15, 58–9,
        60–1
    raised pools 60–1
posts 13, 40–1, 42, 44–5
    pillars 49
    posts and wires 48
pumps 17, 53, 62

R
railway sleepers (railroad
    ties) 11, 60–1

residual current devices
    (RCDs) 19
rock gardens 7, 14, 53
    building 54–5

S
safety 9, 18–19
screwdrivers 17
screws 9, 42, 44, 46, 47
slopes 32, 38, 54, 60
softwood 11, 13
spirit (carpenter's) level 17,
    33, 38, 40, 41, 42, 45,
    58, 59
stone 14, 38, 54, 60
    paving 10, 19

T
tools 17, 18–19
trellis 7, 13, 44
    arbours 43
    fixing to wall 50
trowels 17, 32

W
walls 6, 7, 12, 37, 38–9, 40,
    50, 51
water features 7, 18–19, 53
    cascades 7, 53
    fountains 53, 62–3
    ponds 6, 7, 14–15, 56–7,
        58–9, 60–1
wire supports 48, 51

The publisher would like to thank
Peter McHoy for supplying the
pictures on pages 28–9 and 56–7.